I0087672

THE BEST EVER
BRIEF HISTORY OF THE

Boston Red Sox

BY
DAVE McGRAIL

Copyright © 2020 by David McGrail

Crebblehawk Press
New York, New York

All rights reserved. No part of this publication may be reproduced, stored in a retrieval system, or transmitted, in any form or by any means, electronic, mechanical, photocopying, recording, or otherwise, without the prior written permission of the author.

Topps® trading cards used courtesy of The Topps Company, Inc.

ISBN: 978-1-7355900-1-1

Cover and Interior Design by Tami Boyce
www.tamiboyce.com

Printed in the United States of America

To Alexa, Siri, and Lauren.

TABLE OF CONTENTS

ACKNOWLEDGMENTS

My deepest gratitude to my fantastic editor, good friend, and partner-in-crime on various projects, Catherine Milligan.

Special thanks to the kids who read and commented on the many drafts of the book. If you want a brutally honest opinion, just ask an eight-year-old.

A BRIEF HISTORY OF BOSTON

*B*oston is the capital of Massachusetts. It has a population of about 700,000, and its entire history can be summarized in one word: brrrrr. My cousin Paul lives right outside of Boston, and he once jumped off of his roof into snow that had piled up eight feet high. Don't believe me? You can check out the video online by searching for "Boston Cousin Paul Jumps Off Roof Into Snow."

Okay, I lied. There is a lot more to Boston than cold winters and also a lot more to Paul. (This is not the last we'll hear about Paul.)

The abridged (shortened) history of Boston goes a little like this. Various Native American tribes, including the Massachusett, the Wampanoag, and the

1

Narragansett, resided for thousands of years around the area we now call Boston. They were minding their own business when the Puritans came ashore in the 1600s and formed the Massachusetts Bay Colony. The Puritans were not particularly fun—sports, recreation, and cards were strictly forbidden—and they were intolerant of other religions.

But they sure knew how to build a city from scratch, and by the mid-1700s Boston was flourishing—not just surviving but thriving. Who needs video games when you can buy whale oil to heat your one-room house and then go to Boston Commons to push a wooden hoop with a stick? Yeah, life was good. But that was about to change. (Read that last sentence in a deep, scary voice. Go ahead, try it again. I can wait.)

Though Massachusetts was still an English colony, Bostonians had a strong independent streak, and when King George decided to tax them in the 1760s and 1770s, they reacted by covering British officers in tar and feathers, dumping British tea into the Boston Harbor, and eventually starting a little thing called the American Revolution in 1775.

Led by John Hancock, Paul Revere, and a bunch of people with the last name "Adams," the Boston militia, known as the Minutemen, figured out pretty quickly that their best chance of winning against the better-equipped British was to fire at them and then quickly retreat before they could counterattack.

The other colonies joined in, and after eight years of fighting, we won the war. And the rest is history ... that you're going to have to learn somewhere else, because now it's time to get to the Boston Red Sox!

"RED SOX"?
REALLY?

*B*oston's American League team was formed in 1901. At that time, Boston also had a National League team, and it decided to remove red dye from its socks, fearing it could infect the players if they got cut. The American League team owner, John Taylor, saw an opportunity. Apparently not believing (or caring?) that his players could die from dye, Taylor announced that Boston's American League team would not follow in the National League team's footsteps, so to speak. His team would wear red socks boldly and be known as the Boston Red Sox.

I don't know about you, but I can't help but wonder whether any Red Sox players ever died from infection caused by red dye. So I asked Siri.

She responded, unhelpfully, "Here's the roster for the Red Sox."

I asked Alexa, and she responded, not surprisingly, "Sorry, I'm not sure about that."

I asked Lauren and she responded, quite typically, "What nonsense is coming out of your mouth this time, Dave?" Lauren is my wife of twenty years. She has been through a lot.

RED SOX THROUGH THE YEARS

*a*ny history of the Red Sox must make mention of baseball's oldest stadium, Fenway Park, which was built in 1912. Fenway Park is famous for The Green Monster—a giant green wall in left field, not a goblin that hides under seats and steals your popcorn when you aren't looking. If you ever visit Fenway Park, you might notice a special red seat in the upper right field bleachers. That marks the longest home run ever hit at Fenway Park, launched into the stands by Ted Williams on June 9, 1946. It measured 502 feet.

The Red Sox won the World Series in 1903, 1912, 1915, 1916, and 1918. Their star player in the '15, '16, and '18 World Series was none other than Babe Ruth (a.k.a. The Bambino), who *pitched* a total of twenty-nine-and-two-thirds scoreless innings.

Okay, before going further, I should confess something. I am a New York Yankees fan. Nevertheless, I promise to be objective and to give the Boston Red Sox credit where credit is due. There is only one caveat: I refuse to write anything about Red Sox player Wade Boggs other than this one sentence you are currently reading. (To find out why, you will have to read *The Best Ever Brief History of the New York Yankees*.) Before the Sox start getting any credit, though, let's talk about the famous Curse of the Bambino.

On January 5, 1920, the Red Sox traded Babe Ruth to the New York Yankees, supposedly so that the Sox owner could use the money from the trade to pay for the production of a Broadway musical. Thereafter, the Red Sox were "cursed" and did not win another World Series for 86 years. And the musical turned out to be a flop, too!

They did almost win the World Series in 1986 against the New York Mets. In fact, they were only one out away. But, in the bottom of the 10th inning of Game 6, Mets batter Mookie Wilson hit a groundball to Red Sox first baseman Bill Buckner. The ball rolled through Buckner's legs, and the Red Sox lost the game and the World Series.

The reality is Buckner had a great career overall—20 seasons and over 2,700 hits—so it's a shame that he is remembered for this one moment. (And I am sorry, all ye Red Sox fans, for the reminder of that tragic loss. I know some parts of history can be painful to face!) Actually, Buckner's not entirely to blame, as Red Sox pitching gave up three straight hits and a wild pitch to set the stage for Mookie Wilson.

That said, I urge you to look up "Bill Buckner Classic" online immediately. It's far more entertaining than watching the moon landing.

The Curse of the Bambino was finally broken in 2004, when the Red Sox beat the Yankees in the American League Championship Series after trailing 3-0 in the series and 4-3 in the ninth inning of Game 4 against Hall-of-Fame closer Mariano Rivera. Heroic plays from David Ortiz and Curt Shilling then propelled the team into the World Series, where they swept the St. Louis Cardinals. The Red Sox won again in 2007, beating the Colorado Rockies. In 2013, the Red Sox beat the St. Louis Cardinals again. David Ortiz batted .688 and was the World Series MVP. Five years later, in 2018, the Red Sox were the best team in baseball, with an incredible 108–54 regular season record, and they prevailed over the Los Angeles Dodgers to win the World Series.

Winning four World Series championships between 2004 and 2018 is pretty impressive. The Yankees won only one World Series during this same period.

See? I swallowed my Yankees pride and gave the Red Sox credit where credit is due. And, yes, I'll admit it pained me. But, like a shot in the arm, it hurt only for a moment. The important truth is that great baseball is always worth celebrating, right? (Just please don't read this section of the book ever again!)

The Red Sox have had a lot of great players and great role models over the years, so selecting only six to focus on is a challenge. My apologies to you, Jim Rice and Dennis Eckersley. Don't worry, though, it's not like I'm going to choose someone like Kevin Youkilis over you. Who would think of doing such a thing?

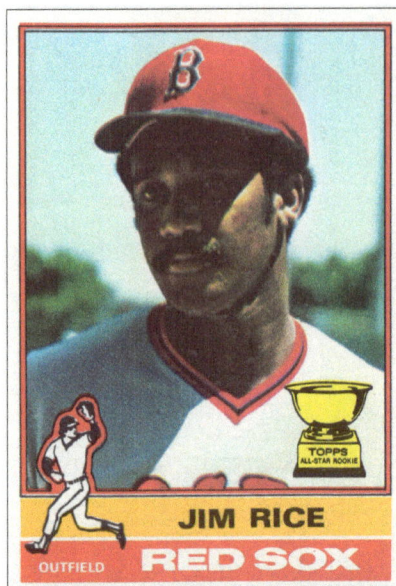

JIM RICE

OUTFIELD **RED SOX**

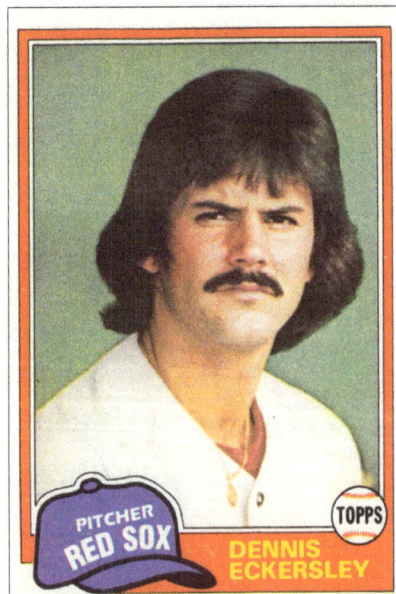

PITCHER
RED SOX

DENNIS ECKERSLEY

TOPPS

CY YOUNG

$\mathcal{F}$or context, I have to tell you first that the active leader for most complete games is Justin Verlander, with 26. Now get this: Cy Young tossed **749** complete games. He is also baseball's all-time leader in wins (511), innings pitched (7,356), and batters faced (29,565).

Young had a 2.00 ERA while pitching for Boston from 1901-1908 and a 2.63 ERA over his 22-year career. He won at least thirty games in five seasons and led the league in fewest walks per nine innings ... fourteen times!

Given these incredible statistics, it is altogether fitting that each year the best pitcher in each league is given the "Cy Young Award." Not to take anything away from Dennis "Oil Can" Boyd, who was a solid Red Sox pitcher in the 1980s, but the "Oil Can Boyd Award" simply doesn't have the same ring to it. Since

I don't have a Cy Young baseball card, though, here's good ol' Oil Can:

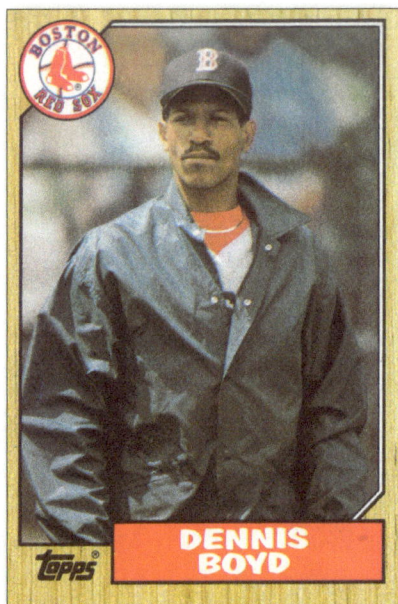

DENNIS BOYD

285 | DENNIS BOYD • PITCHER

COMPLETE MAJOR LEAGUE PITCHING RECORD

YR CLUB	G	IP	W	L	R	ER	SO	BB	ES	CG	SHO	SV	ERA
82 RED SOX	3	8.1	0	1	5	5	2	2	1	0	0	0	5.40
83 RED SOX	15	98.2	4	8	46	36	43	23	13	5	0	0	3.28
84 RED SOX	29	197.2	12	12	109	96	134	53	26	10	3	0	4.37
85 RED SOX	35	272.1	15	13	117	112	154	67	35	13	3	0	3.70
86 RED SOX	30	214.1	16	10	99	90	129	45	30	10	0	0	3.78
MAJ. LEA. TOTALS	112	791.1	47	44	376	339	462	190	105	38	6	0	3.86

Dennis attended Jackson State University (Jackson, Miss.). His popular nickname is "Oil Can".

♦ ♦ ♦ ♦ ♦ ♦ ♦ ON THIS DATE ♦ ♦ ♦ ♦ ♦ ♦ ♦
May 20, 1962: Ken Hubbs collected 8 singles in doubleheader for Cubs. Ken's 1962 Topps card was #461.

® © 1987 TOPPS CHEWING GUM, INC. PRTD. IN U.S.A.

HT: 6'1" WT: 165 THROWS: RIGHT BATS: RIGHT DRFT: RED SOX #16-JUNE, 1980.
ACQ: VIA DRAFT BORN: 10-6-59, MERIDIAN, MISS. HOME: MERIDIAN, MISS.

TED WILLIAMS

*O*n September 1, 1939, Germany invaded Poland, and World War II was officially underway. The United States stayed out of the war at first but meanwhile sent food, oil, supplies, airplanes, and weapons to England and other European countries to help in the war effort. It entered the war after the Japanese bombed Pearl Harbor in Hawaii on December 7, 1941, a date that I hope will stick in your mind like slime on a carpet.

Wait, how is this relevant to the Boston Red Sox?! I'm glad you asked.

Ted Williams voluntarily enlisted in the Navy as a pilot and, because of his patriotic service, missed the 1943-45 baseball seasons. It should come as no surprise that Williams set Navy training records in reflexes, coordination, and visual reaction time. What's more, while he did not experience direct combat in World War II, he did fight as a Marine pilot in the Korean War a few years later, barely escaping death on a number of occasions.

Nicknamed the "Splendid Splinter," Williams spent five years of his baseball career in the military. Keeping this in mind, his career statistics will blow you away:

- Nineteen-time All-Star
- Two-time Triple Crown winner
- 521 career home runs
- .344 career batting average
- .482 career on-base percentage, the highest in MLB history

Think about that last statistic. Williams got on base about half of the times he went to bat!

Williams's 1941 season deserves special recognition. That year he led the league in home runs, runs, on-base percentage, and slugging percentage. He also led the majors with a .406 batting average, marking the last time in MLB history that a player hit .400.

There will never be another player like Ted Williams. There may, however, be the *same* Ted Williams someday, since he had his body frozen after he died. I'm not kidding.

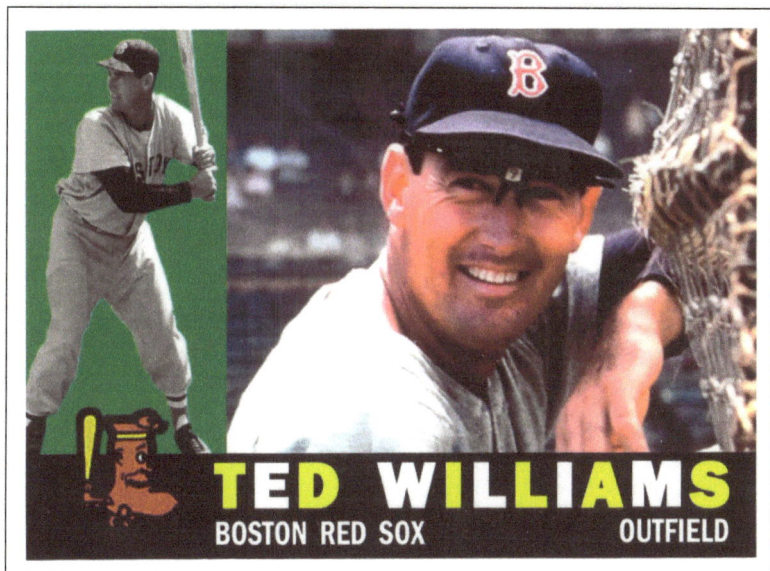

TED WILLIAMS
BOSTON RED SOX   OUTFIELD

PEDRO MARTINEZ

*P*edro Martinez's career numbers are incredible: he boasts the sixth highest winning percentage in MLB history, over 3,000 strikeouts, and a 2.93 ERA.

From 1997-2003, Martinez was by far the most dominant pitcher in baseball, and for most of those years he was with the Red Sox. During this period, he won three Cy Young Awards (1997, 1999, 2000) and was runner-up twice (1998, 2002), while also leading the league in ERA five times and posting a 118–36 record. And he did this pitching in the American League (with the designated hitter) at Fenway Park—a great ballpark for left-handed hitters—during a period when many hitters were, um, stronger than usual.

When he was elected to the Hall of Fame in 2015, Martinez said, "I cannot be any prouder to take the

Red Sox Nation to the Hall of Fame with the logo on my plaque."

Pedro Martinez was fun-loving and fun to watch. His charitable foundation seeks to improve the lives of kids in the Dominican Republic, where Martinez grew up. The foundation's website is www.pedromartinezfoundation.com. Check it out.

KEVIN YOUKILIS

*Y*es, Kevin Youkilis. Because it's my book and I have plenty to say about Kevin Youkilis, far more than about Jim Rice or Dennis Eckersley!

Youkilis played for the Red Sox from 2004-2012. He will never be in the Hall of Fame, but he has two World Series rings while Ted Williams had zero, so you tell me who should be in the Hall? Well, okay, probably Williams. But still.

There is a lot more to Youkilis than meets the eye.

First, Youkilis was nicknamed "The Greek God of Walks" in Michael Lewis's best-selling book, *Moneyball*, where Lewis concluded that, statistically, Youkilis was one of the most valuable players in baseball because of his patience at the plate.

Second, Youkilis had one of the most bizarre batting stances ever. Search "Youkilis Crazy" online and you'll see what I mean.

Third, my cousin Paul (Remember him? The guy who jumped off of his roof into the Boston snow?) met Youkilis in a bar after the Red Sox won the World Series in 2007. Paul knows the Red Sox better than anyone on earth, and there was a lot he was eager to discuss with Youkilis. But, alas, he found himself starstruck, and somehow the only words he could muster were a barely audible, "Thank you." To Paul's son, Nolan—I'm sorry you had to hear this from me.

Fourth, Kevin Youkilis is married to Julie Brady. Julie Brady (@DestroyBaseball) is an interesting person. As far as I can tell, she's into baseball, politics, philosophy, and making a difference in her community. She seems really cool. I would have an apple juice with her ... but only if it wouldn't upset Youkilis, who scares me. Or her brother, Tom Brady.

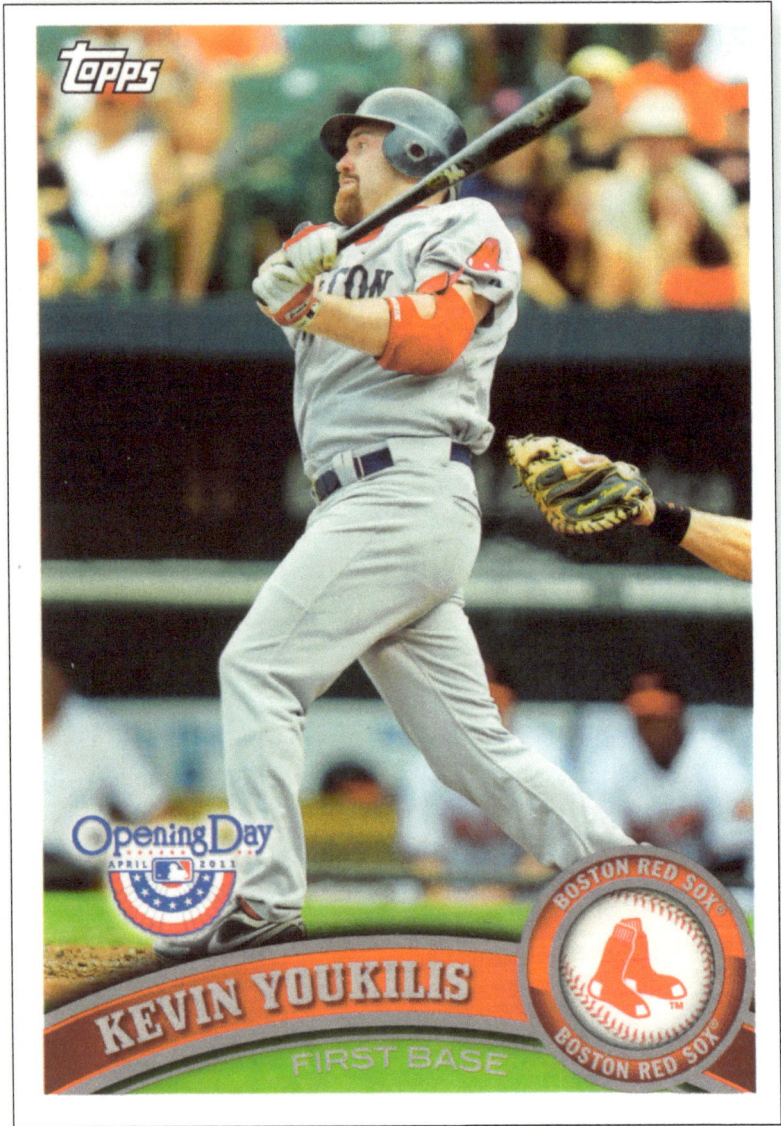

DUSTIN PEDROIA

*D*ustin Pedroia began his career with the Red Sox in 2006. He's a four-time All-Star and Gold Glove Winner and was named the American League MVP in 2008, when he collected 118 runs, 213 hits, and 54 doubles. He helped the Red Sox win the World Series in 2007 and 2013.

The Red Sox officially list Pedroia at 5 feet 9 inches. My response: HAHAHAHAHAHAHA. If Pedroia is a fraction of an inch above 5'7", then I'm a monkey's uncle. Don't worry, Joey, I'm not calling you a monkey. (Joey is my nephew.)

How is it possible that a guy that size, who looks like he should be a painter's apprentice, has excelled in the majors?

Neuroscience, which is the study of the brain, provides the answer. It turns out that Pedroia's brain has been studied and that he has extraordinary reaction time, hand-eye coordination, inhibitory control, and spin recognition, even better than most MLB players, who tend to excel in these skills. In the 0.4 seconds it takes a Major League fastball to reach home plate after it leaves a pitcher's hand, Pedroia has an almost super-human ability to figure out what's coming his way and react accordingly.

It also doesn't hurt that he has 20/10 vision. To give you some idea of what that means, "perfect" vision is 20/20. If you stand about nine feet away from the next page you'd have to be able to read the seventh line to have 20/10 vision.

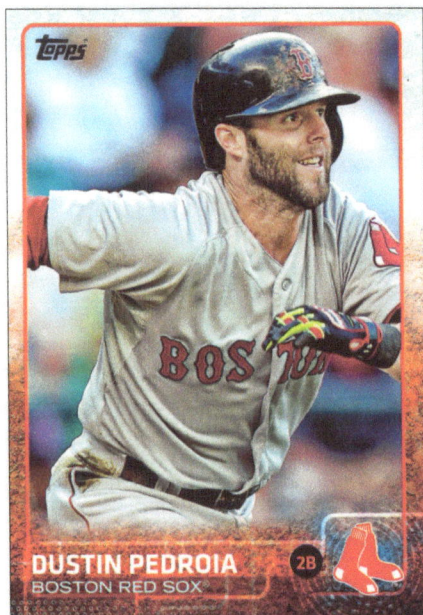

D

US

TIN

PLAYS

BASEBALL

MAYBEHEALSO

PAINTSHISHOUSE

MOOKIE BETTS

*M*ookie Betts began his career with the Boston Red Sox in 2014. He was an All Star from 2016-2019 and the American League MVP in 2018, when he batted a league-leading .346 and scored a league-leading 129 runs, with 30 stolen bases. He led the Red Sox to their 2018 World Series title over the Los Angeles Dodgers.

Moreover, Betts is really likable—just watch him in any post-game interview. His smile is infectious. He clearly loves the game and inspires teammates and fans alike.

A career .301 hitter, Mookie Betts is destined be a superstar and the face of the Red Sox organization for years to come. Wait, what's that? THE RED SOX TRADED BETTS TO THE DODGERS IN 2020?!

I'm not superstitious, but when you win a World Series in '18 and then trade your best player, whose name happens to be *Mookie*, no less, aren't you basically inviting a new curse? Better a curse than a virus, but still ...

At least the great city of Boston will always have Tom Brady. Wait, WHAT?!

MOOKIE BETTS

ONE UNBELIEVABLE
RED SOX MOMENT

Do you ever pretend it's the bottom of the ninth in Game 7 of the World Series, tie game? Boston catcher and future Hall-of-Famer Carlton Fisk basically lived this dream at 12:33 a.m. on October 22, 1975, when he stepped to the plate at Fenway Park in Game 6 of the World Series, with the score tied at six and the Red Sox down three games to two against the Cincinnati Reds.

Fisk recalled that, before he stepped to the plate, Pete Rose (who ultimately retired with 4,256 hits, more than any other player, and is not in the Hall of Fame—a topic for another book) said to him, "This is the greatest game ever."

Fisk then did what every young baseball player hopes he can someday do: he launched a home run to win the game. The Fenway crowd went crazy and stormed the field. But it almost didn't happen, because the ball was hooking foul. Fisk hopped up and down as he headed toward first, waving his arms, willing the ball to stay fair. Then, when he knew the ball was fair, he kept jumping for joy as he rounded the bases. This was a grown man acting like an 8-year-old. It was wonderful to watch, but it turns out that the only reason we saw Fisk's reaction was because the cameraman had a huge rat near his feet and couldn't follow the path of the ball, so he kept the camera on Fisk.

It was undoubtedly one of the greatest moments in sports history. Now that you've read about it, look up "Must C Carlton Fisk" online and enjoy!

Carlton Fisk: The Wave

THE BEST RED SOX BASEBALL CARD EVER

I would like to introduce you to Jerry Remy's moustache. It is attached to former Red Sox second baseman Jerry Remy, now a terrific broadcaster who has been calling Sox games since 1988. I'm hoping he has a sense of humor.

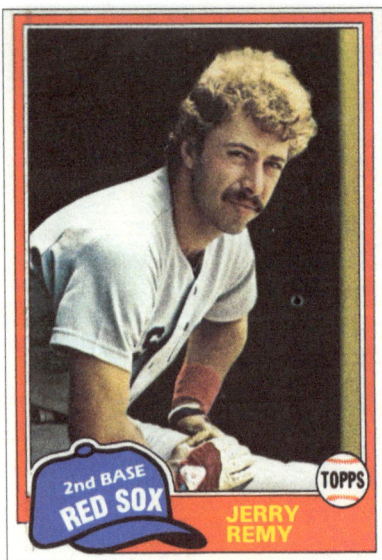

www.ingramcontent.com/pod-product-compliance
Lightning Source LLC
Chambersburg PA
CBHW040348060426
42445CB00030B/154